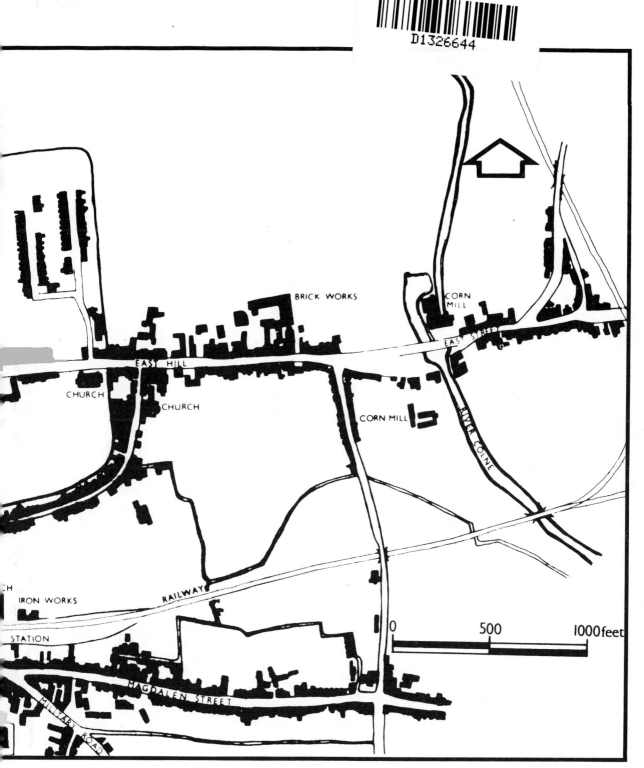

BRICK WORKS

CORN MILL

EAST STREET

EAST HILL

CHURCH

CHURCH

CORN MILL

RIVER COLNE

RAILWAY

IRON WORKS

STATION

MAGDALEN STREET

MILITARY ROAD

0   500   1000 feet

Victorian Colchester, taken from an Ordnance Survey map of 1875.

COLCHESTER
A Pictorial History

View of High Street and the *Three Cups Hotel*.

COLCHESTER
A Pictorial History

John Marriage

Phillimore

1988

Published by
PHILLIMORE & CO. LTD.
Shopwyke Hall, Chichester, Sussex

© John Marriage, 1988

ISBN 0 85033 662 7

Printed and bound by
BIDDLES LTD.
Guildford, Surrey

List of Illustrations

The Town

1. High Street, 1857
2. High Street after the demolition of Middle Row
3. A map of the town in 1803
4. High Street in Edwardian times
5. High Street, 1910
6. & 7. Two views of High Street in about 1908
8. High Street *c.*1925, seen from East Hill
9. The 'Siege House'
10. Siege House, *c.*1930
11. Hythe Hill near its junction with Port Lane
12. The junction of Magdalen Street and Military Road in 1897
13. The ruins of St Botolph's Priory
14. St Botolph's Street, *c.*1910
15. The 15th-century gatehouse to St John's Abbey
16. Trinity Street
17. Scheregate Steps, *c.*1910
18. Long Wyre Street
19. Pelhams Lane, *c.*1910
20. The Victorian water tower, 'Jumbo'
21. St Mary's steps, Balkerne Hill, 1824
22. Head Street
23. Headgate early this century
24. Lexden Road in 1904
25. North Hill at the High Street junction, *c.*1910
26. Pony and trap, *c.*1910
27. Looking up North Hill

Commerce

28. No. 11 High Street
29. Co-operative Society's shop in Long Wyre Street
30. Interior of the Co-operative Society's shop, *c.*1925
31. A 1930's lingerie display by the Co-operative Society
32. & 33. James Dace & Son
34. A young Arthur Hatfield in 1920
35. Arthur Hatfield with his assistants
36. A 1928 advertisement
37. The *Red Lion Hotel*, *c.*1900
38. The *Castle Inn*
39. The *Stockwell Arms*
40. Italianate hotel at North Station
41. The Capital and Counties Bank
42. The banking chamber at No. 17 High Street
43. The interior of Barclays Bank in 1930
44. 19th-century bank notes of Colchester Bank
45. The Parr Bank Ltd.
46. Cattle market scene, 1900
47. An 1865 advertisement for artificial teeth

Residential Colchester

48. West Stockwell Street, *c.*1950
49. West Stockwell Street earlier this century
50. The lower part of the street during the inter-war period
51. 'Deoban', Lexden Road
52. Model displayed on Co-operators Day in 1924
53. Electricity advertisement

Schools

54. Colchester Royal Grammar School
55. The original Technical School buildings
56. A 1909 school report
57. Book given as a prize
58. Pupils of Group XXI, Canterbury Road School

Open Spaces

59. Colchester Castle, 1824
60. Colchester Castle
61. Castle Park
62. Lower Castle Park at the turn of the century
63. Middle Mill, *c.*1927
64. The millpond at Middle Mill
65. Bridge over the River Colne in Castle Park

Industry

66. Bourne Mill
67. East Mill in 1840
68. East Mill in 1883
69. East Mill in 1940
70. A facsimile of Marriage's 3lb linen flour bag
71. A steam pump
72. An ultrasonic steam boiler
73. A lathe built in 1890 by the Britannia Engineering Company
74. Aerial photograph of The Hythe
75. Drying lucerne at Frank Pertwee & Sons
76. A dust extractor
77. Benjamin Cant's 1865 advertisement for plants
78. The interior of the Colchester Lathe Company's factory
79. The 'Mascot'

Transport

80. The schooner *Essex Lass* of Colchester
81. & 82. Two views of The Hythe in about 1900
83. The Hythe, *c.*1950
84. The Thames sailing barge *Dawn* at East Mills
85. *Dawn* passing under Hythe Bridge
86. The *Signality* photographed about 1950

87. The first train from Ipswich in 1846
88. The exterior of the original North Station buildings
89. A London-bound G.E.R. train
90. The 11.30 a.m. Colchester to Clacton goods train
91. A G.E.R. locomotive
92. A tram, c.1910
93. A corporation employee ready to change the tramway points
94. A tram approaching Station terminus
95. Tram driver and conductor
96. An open-decked bus, 1929
97. Bus outside the Essex and Suffolk Equitable building
98. A Moore Brothers' bus, c.1920
99. The interior of the Eastern National bus garage
100. The old bus park in St John's Street, c.1950
101. Advertisement for bus and train tickets
102. Bus take-over notification
103. Moore Brothers of Kelvedon
104. Co-operative Society's working horses
105. Frank Pertwee and Sons' lorry fleet
106. Wrights' new lorry, 1920
107. Advertisement from a 1928 guide to the town

Public Buildings
108. The Town Hall
109. Plans of The Town Hall, 1897
110. First public library
111. Second public library
112. Colchester and Essex County Hospital
113. The new children's ward
114. The exterior of the children's ward
115. The staff of the Colchester Union Workhouse, 1898
116. St Nicholas church, c.1910
117. Culver Street Methodist church
118. Trinity Church
119. Trinity Church doorway

Military Colchester
120. The Officers' Mess, Hyderabad Barracks
121. A military brass band
122. Artillery training prior to 1914
123. A typical training camp in 1931
124. The Royal Engineers' summer camp, 1912

125. A humorous card, c.1917
126. A studio picture of Gunner Rolly Fisher, May 1916
127. & 128. Two photographs of the Military Hospital
129. Vehicles and drivers of the Army Motor Reserve, c.1906
130. Bomb damage suffered on 21 February 1915

Historic Events
131. The first sailing barge to reach East Mill in 1865
132. Damage from the 1884 earthquake
133. The guard of honour at the official opening of Castle Park, 1892
134. Diamond Jubilee procession down St Botolph's Street
135. Opening of the new tramway system on 28 July 1904
136. The Colchester Fire Brigade, 1906
137. & 138. Colchester pageant, 21 to 26 June 1909
139. & 140. Derailing of the Cromer to Liverpool Street Express on 12 July 1913
141. Unveiling of the War Memorial on Empire Day, 1923
142. The Colchester Carnival, c.1920
143.)
144.} Procession on Co-operators Day 4 July 1924
145.)
146. The Essex County football team in 1907
147. A serious fire in High Street, 1923

Some Colchester People
148. Viscount Cowdray
149. Wilson Marriage
150. H. H. Fisher and Private Harry Marriage in 1917
151. John Hatfield
152. Frank Pertwee in the early 1950s
153. Teddy Grimes and Marmalade Emma
154. Jack Clarke aged 14
155. A Victorian family group
156. The staff of Colchester Corporation Tramways
157. The *Essex County Standard* staff, c.1930
158. The 1926 wedding of Mabel and Harold Peachey

Acknowledgements

The illustrations appear by kind permission of the following: Essex Record Office, 1, 3, 13, 14, 16, 18, 19, 21, 22, 25, 28, 39, 40, 46, 58, 59, 64, 72, 79, 85, 87, 90, 91, 106, 108, 111, 115, 116, 127, 128, 151, 155; Colchester Museum, 2, 11, 12, 113, 130, 131, 132, 134, 145; Mr. L. Whittaker, 5, 6, 23, 37, 93, 107, 133, 137, 138, 142; Mrs. B. Ibbotson, 7, 86, 120; Mr. Bob Drake, 9, 10, 67, 68, 69, 129, 147; Colchester and East Essex Co-operative Society, 29, 30, 31, 52, 102, 139, 140, 141; Hatfield Furnishers, 34, 35, 149; Lloyds Bank, 41, 42; Barclays Bank, 43, 44; National Westminster Bank, 45; Mr. Harry Marriage, 56, 57, 124, 148, 154; Mr. Derek Tripp, 63; Pertwee Holdings Ltd., 74, 75, 76, 81, 103, 150; Passmore Edwards Museum, 82, 83; Mr. A.G. Osborne, 96, 97, 99, 100, 101; Loco Club of Great Britain, 88, 89; Mr. Roy Marshall, 98; Mr. W. J. Haynes, 95; Mr. B. Barnes, 70, 144, 156; Mr. C. Carter, 94, 95. All other illustrations supplied by the author.

Preface

Colchester today is a prosperous and growing town within an equally thriving and expanding area, but it was not always so. In this book I have gathered illustrations of the town during a quieter era from the middle of the last century to 1950, when major redevelopment was still in the future. The motor car had yet to become absolute king of the highway, demanding as the price of its rule major new roads and multi-storey car parks, both of which have drastically changed the landscape.

Although I am an Essex person, I cannot claim to be a native of Colchester but, from childhood, I have been a regular visitor. Its complexity, greater than most comparable provincial communities, has always been a source of interest. Few places can claim to combine the role of university town, garrison town, market town and and port, as well as being noted for industries and shopping, with so long a history.

In the preparation of this book I have received considerable help from many people and I would like to thank those who have kindly lent me their valuable pictures and in particular my father, Harry Marriage, who, as a Colcestrian, has been able to relate, so clearly, his memories of the town as it was in the early years of this century. I must also thank my wife who provided invaluable assistance in the preparation of the text and captions, as well as checking the grammar and spelling.

Historical Introduction

Colchester is without doubt the most interesting town in Essex and it compares favourably with places like St Albans or York for the richness of its heritage. This is perhaps not so surprising when one remembers that it is the oldest recorded town in England. Roman remains abound, there are Saxon traces, plus medieval and later structures. There is also a particular wealth of buildings dating back to Victorian and Edwardian times. In addition to these purely structural relics from the past, the basic road layout, within the perimeter wall, still follows the grid-iron pattern laid down when the Romans established their town.

Prior to the arrival of the Romans in 55 B.C. Colchester was already a Celtic centre, the capital of the kingdom of *Cunobelin* and known as *Camulodonum*. There are, however, few obvious remains of this era.

For defensive reasons Colchester was built on a hill, with the town walls enclosing the higher parts. The present High Street, which aligns with Balkerne Gate, formerly the main entrance to the town, runs along the brow of the hill. Visitors quickly notice the hard slog if they walk from the River Colne up to the modern town centre. The steep slopes they encounter would have helped in the defence of the Roman town. The area enclosed by the Roman walls is about 108 acres. It is not clear whether all the land was built on by the Romans as it was their custom to allow room within the walls for a town to grow and this did not always happen.

Balkerne Gate was imposingly constructed with four arched entrances. Two were 17 feet wide and built for wheeled traffic, whilst the others were each six feet wide and intended for pedestrians. For some reason during the Roman occupation this gate was sealed off and replaced by Head Gate, sited on the south side of the town. In Victorian times rather poor quality houses were built close to it. Now, owing to more recent clearance, its remains make an impressive sight next to the town's modern inner relief road. The later use of Head Gate as a main entrance to the town had an effect on the evolving road layout and even today the road to London still runs from this original site.

Without question the most impressive old building in Colchester is the Castle Keep – popularly known simply as 'The Castle'. The outer walls vanished many years ago. It has the distinction of being the largest keep in the country and, with a ground plan of 151 feet by 110 feet, it is considerably greater than the Tower of London. In building it, the Normans made considerable use of Roman building materials taken from the remains of the earlier town. Much of this material was of poor quality and so it was strengthened with stone especially imported by water from Normandy and the Isle of Wight. Originally the building was much higher, but it was partially demolished in 1683 and the materials re-used elsewhere. Earlier this century the Castle was converted into a museum after being used for a variety of purposes and it now houses an impressive display of Roman and later remains. A unique feature of the Castle is the existence of the substructure of the Temple of Claudius under the massive vaults. This previously occupied the same site and was located in the centre of the Roman town.

A number of other older buildings are also prominent in the centre of the town. Constructed in 1902, following a competition for the best design, the splendid Edwardian Town Hall is sited halfway along the High Street, whilst the Essex and Suffolk Equitable building is located at the junction of North Hill and High Street. The latter was built as the Corn Exchange in 1820 and has a colonnade of Doric columns over the pavement. Ironically, however, the building which has dominated the town for over a century is a Victorian water tower. It was built in 1882 by the Town Council which was responsible for supplying the town with water until Anglian Water took over. The tower is a massive brick structure, with four huge brick legs. It stands at the very crest of Balkerne Hill, close to the original entrance to the Roman town and is affectionately known locally as 'Jumbo', reputedly named after an Indian elephant which was quite a celebrity at London Zoo at the time! The huge iron reservoir, sitting right at the top and holding a quarter of a million gallons of water, was made nearby at the former Mumford's Iron Works in Culver Street. The bricks were also made locally.

There has been a rapid rise in the population of the town since the beginning of the 19th century. In 1801 the population was a mere 11,500. Fifty years later it had risen to 19,000. In 1901 it was 38,000, whilst in 1971 it had reached 76,531, and the expansion continues. This ever increasing population has resulted in a continuing need for more houses, shops, factories and offices, as well as schools and open spaces.

Commerce

Colchester High Street, together with the adjoining roads, has long been a centre for retail trade. Today, the various premises are mostly branches of national chain stores but at the turn of the century almost all shops were owned by individual proprietors who either lived above the shop or, if they were prosperous and successful, in villas conveniently located elsewhere in the town. In those days shops included every trade necessary for day-to-day living. As well as tailors, chemists, drapers and grocers, they included trades long gone such as clothiers, hatters and ice merchants – the latter essential for food preservation before the days of refrigeration. Providing for the substantial military presence in the town was another aspect of commercial life.

One name still familiar today was Henry Griffin, described in 1890 as a cabinet maker and upholsterer. He was, of course, the forerunner of the present day firm of Williams and Griffin. His shop was described in contemporary advertisements as being 'spacious'. It was about 50 feet in length and possessed two windows. In each 'there are always beautiful articles of furniture etc. Drawing, dining, morning and bedroom suites are here to be seen in great variety and there is a large stock of painted furniture, Chippendale furniture'. His patrons were drawn from the 'upper classes'.

Another firm going back to the same era is Hatfields Furnishers, now moved from the town centre to Peartree Lane. The founder of the firm was John Hatfield, who in 1886 was a 'Dealer in curios', using the front room of his house at No. 31 St John's Street to do business. In 1916 his youngest son, Arthur, joined the firm, and Nos. 32-34 St John's Street were added. Sales, in season, included grapes, grown in a greenhouse at the rear, and sold at ½d a pound! Their warehouse on the opposite side of the road was acquired and demolished by the Council to make way for a bus park (subsequently redeveloped as a multi-storey car park) thus creating a busier location for the shop. This proved too much for Arthur Hatfield to handle and he promptly moved to a quieter location in Stanwell Street where a miscellaneous collection of secondhand goods accumulated. Upon the arrival of Arthur's son-in-law, the more ambitious John London, who joined the firm in 1945 after war service in the R.A.F., the character of the firm began to change. He gradually took over its management and was soon helped by his younger brother, Tony. Hardware was stocked for the first time and new furniture starting with the famous brand, Parker Knoll. Eventually, with further expansion in mind, the firm moved to Peartree Lane.

On 13 May 1861, just 17 years after the first Co-operative shop in Rochdale had opened, a general meeting was held in Colchester to draw up rules for a Colchester co-operative society. A committee of 28 was formed and by 9 August a special meeting of members was held in Culver Street, on the premises of John Taylor of the *Essex Standard*, to mark the opening of the first shop. At first the shop sold only bread and flour. Later, butter, sugar, cheese, soap, soda, and starch, blues, blacking, black lead and mustard were added to the stock. The first balance sheet showed sales of £429, assets of nearly £89, and the dividend was declared at a shilling in the pound. An educational committee was formed in 1865 and enthusiastically pioneered a programme of activities based upon the co-operative ideals of self improvement, self help, sharing and comradeship in action. In 1890 the Colchester Co-operative Women's Guild was formed and lending libraries, reading rooms, choirs, drama groups, children's clubs, exhibitions, outings, talks and conferences were organised. From these small beginnings, the Colchester and East Essex Co-operative Society has developed into one of the most successful in the country, with over 100,000 members and over 1,400 employees.

Colchester has long been an important market town, serving the surrounding rural area. Originally the market was held in the High Street, with corn and cattle sales each Saturday and fruit and poultry each Wednesday. In those times St Runwald's church and Middle Row still stood in the centre of High Street and there is no doubt that High Street must have been very congested on market days. After a short-lived attempt to transfer the cattle market to a site near Balkerne Hill, in 1862 it moved to land at the bottom of North Hill, previously occupied by a tannery, and remained there for over a century. More recently it has again moved, this time to Wyncolls Road to make way for modern redevelopment. However, the ever popular retail market remains in High Street, the stalls creating a picturesque and busy atmosphere. Every Saturday bargains can be purchased from the wide variety of goods on sale at the kerbside.

The Victorian era saw the establishment of the modern banking system and branches of national banks opened in the town. In 1899, the Capital and Counties Bank opened a small office at No. 97 High Street and in 1901, with business expanding rapidly, they moved to larger premises at No.17 High Street. Seventeen years later it amalgamated with Lloyds Bank and by 1926 had again outgrown its accommodation. A site was acquired nearby at No. 27 High Street, the existing building being demolished and replaced by a neo-Georgian-style building – typical of bank buildings of the time. Somewhat surprisingly, the first floor was occupied by a café.

In 1774 Crickett & Co. opened an office in High Street and became known as the Colchester Bank. One of the original partners was Mr. Waley, who also helped to run the Colchester wine and spirit firm of Waley and Desbrosscs. The Bank had its ups and downs and there were particularly anxious moments when their London agents Esdaile & Co. crashed. However, another firm, Barnetts, Hoare & Co., helped out by sending Joseph Hoare to Colchester with a substantial sum of money. During Queen Victoria's reign the Colchester Bank gained a reputation for solidarity and in 1891, when another local bank, Mills Bawtree, failed, it was able to provide funds for the distressed customers. In 1896 the

Colchester Bank joined forces with Barclays & Co. as part of an amalgamation of some 20 private banks. It became Barclays Bank Ltd. in 1917.

The forerunner of the present National Westminster Bank, now located at No. 25 High Street, goes back to 1852 with the opening of the London & County Bank, although it is uncertain whether trading was on the present site. However, the present substantial Edwardian structure dates back to 1902 and its construction was marked by the find of some 2,000 early English silver coins in a lead casket, whilst the footings were being dug. Their owner was clearly anticipating the future use of the site as a location for the safe keeping of valuables! Two of the coins have found their way into the bank's records.

The *Old Red Lion Hotel* has long been familiar to Colcestrians. In 1890 the proprietor was an H. Heath and in his advertisement he described the hotel as being 'the resort of families visiting the town as well as commercial gentlemen'. It was said to have the 'usual public rooms, including coffee rooms, ladies drawing room, smoke room', all furnished in a 'superior manner'. An omnibus, presumably horse-drawn, met all trains and, in addition, saddle horses were available at any time. The *Old Red Lion*, however, was but one of a wealth of hotels, inns and public houses which existed in the centre of the town. Another hotel of similar calibre was *The George*, which had the famous trademark, 'you can always get a lobster at *The George*'. The trade for all these licensed premises was drawn not only from townspeople and visitors, but, of course, the soldiers from the barracks who had money, especially on pay day, to liven up the long dark evenings. Many inns had their roots back in the old coaching days, although others were simple beer houses. The number of inns and public houses has fallen steadily throughout the century and many have either been demolished or converted to other uses as trade declined.

Before radio and television reduced the demand for live productions, Colchester could boast a variety of entertainments. The Theatre Royal was built in Queens Street in 1812 and over the years many famous artistes trod the boards and it became a popular venue for the professional classes and, once the garrison was permanently established, very prosperous. Another theatre, the Hippodrome, opened in High Street in 1904 with seating for nearly 1,500 people. For a brief period intense rivalry existed between the two, until the Theatre Royal was destroyed by fire in 1918.

The 1930s and the '40s were the golden age of the cinema when film going was a weekly event for most people. At one time five cinemas existed; only two, however, were specifically built as such, the Odeon in Crouch Street, built in 1933 as the Regal, and the old Electric Cinema in St John's Street.

Residential Colchester

One of the earliest residential areas in the town is the so-called 'Dutch' quarter to the north of High Street and east of North Hill on land falling steeply towards the river. It was established mainly in the 16th century by Flemish weavers who were fleeing the Spanish persecution of Protestants in the Netherlands and many of the properties still date back to those days. A considerable number were restored in early post-war years.

Later developments to the town included large areas of Victorian houses north of Crouch Street and along Barrack Street towards the Hythe. These were built to minimum housing standards in long straight terraces, although many have attractive detailing. Evocative of the former occupation of the land by the army are roads like Artillery Street and Cannon Street. At the same time as these artisan houses were being built, spacious detached villas were erected along Lexden Road for the wealthy and professional classes.

Inter-war houses were built on the periphery of the town and it was during this time that Mile End, formerly a separate village, developed as a suburb of Colchester with a large Council estate. Other development took place at Lexden and Old Heath. It is perhaps unfortunate that the town's first bypass, constructed in the late 1920s as a three-lane road, soon became lined with a ribbon of speculative houses which, in creating their own traffic needs, rapidly reduced the value of the new bypass as a through route from London to Ipswich and the seaside towns.

Schools
In Victorian times the Church of England and the Methodist Church played a prominent part in the provision of elementary education through the foundation of 'National' and 'British' schools respectively. Later on the Council began to play an increasingly important part. In those times there was a concentrated effort on the 'Three R's' – Reading, (W)riting and (A)rithmetic – and a strong classroom discipline meant that scholastic standards were remarkably high, even if the classes were large and the buildings often cramped.

The Colchester School Board was established in 1892 and commenced a programme of school building, particularly urgent in view of the rising population. These included a school at North Street and the two- and three-storied Barrack Street School, opened in 1894 and intended to accommodate 1,200 children. The school was later renamed the Wilson Marriage School in honour of a former Mayor of the town and a frequent visitor to the school. Other schools were built at Canterbury Road, Mile End and East Ward.

Secondary education for the fortunate few was provided by the old established Colchester Royal Grammar School. Once it was located in Culver Street, but in 1853 it moved to a new site in Lexden Road near the hospital. Since then the school has greatly expanded but the original headmaster's house and schoolroom, now the school library, remain. Later on, secondary education was also provided by the North East Essex Technical College and School of Art and the County High School for Girls, but it was not until the passing of the Education Act of 1944 that secondary education became available to everyone. This act resulted in a crash programme of school building.

Recreation
The town's first public open space at the junction of Old Heath Road and Wimpole Road was rather unimaginatively named simply 'The Recreation Ground'. Inevitably it was to become known by generations of Colcestrians as just 'The Rec'. Earlier it had been part of a large parade field for the army and it was released by the military authorities in 1885. To this day it remains a rather dull, flat, open area of land. In October 1892, the far more impressive and interesting Castle Park was opened. This was augmented by the opening of the lower park in March 1893. In 1920 the Castle itself, together with the adjacent Holly Trees Mansion, was purchased by Viscount Cowdray and presented to the town. With the Castle at its centre, its mature trees and undulating slopes down to the River Colne, this open space is perhaps one of the finest public parks in the county.

Industry
Colchester, like most other provincial country towns, has a long tradition of industry. Originally it served the needs of the townspeople and the surrounding rural area together with other places accessible via the tidal estuary. Most of these firms were small and

included flour mills, breweries, tanneries, rope manufactories and various foundries. They tended to be scattered haphazardly throughout the back streets and yards in the older parts of the town. Those industries which required the use of water, either as a source of power or as part of their processing, were of course sited on or near the River Colne or streams. Later, expanding industrial development with a wider market requiring the use of bulk transportation, either for the raw material or the finished product or both, grew up around The Hythe, using barges or the developing rail network. From about 1920 firms began to reduce their dependence on rail or water and increasingly moved their goods by road. Newer industries were likely therefore to grow up next to roads rather than the estuary or the railway.

Bourne Mill (built in 1591) was one of the earlier examples of an industry obtaining its power from running water. It is located on Bourne Brook, a tributary of the Colne. This building is now owned and preserved by the National Trust. Other examples were Middle Mill and East Mills. All three ground flour, most of which was sold in the town. Middle Mill, sometimes known as Choppings Mill after its owner, was demolished by the Borough Council after it had been used for several years as a park store. A simple weir adjacent to Castle Park marks its site. In 1840 East Mills was purchased by Edward Marriage from Chelmsford. In those days it was a traditional corn mill drawing water from the River Colne to turn its wheels. In 1872 Edward Marriage's son, Wilson, became a partner and under his forceful management the character of the mill began to change. In 1883 the water wheels and part of the original buildings were replaced by a steam roller plant and in 1890 it doubled in size and output, replacing the remainder of the original building by a duplicate roller plant. Much of its produce was destined to be sold elsewhere, cargoes being transported by water and rail. Later on road haulage took over. The firm celebrated its centenary in 1940, only to disappear shortly afterwards within the giant Hovis-Rank-MacDougall milling combine. The mill is now closed and the main building, which housed the steam roller plant, has been converted into a hotel.

Brewing was also a substantial local industry. Firms existing at the turn of the century included the Colchester Brewing Company, which had premises at East Hill. This took over the neighbouring firm of Charrington Nicholls and in return was swallowed up by Ind Coope, a national company whose nearest brewery is at Romford. A mineral water offshoot of Nicholls survived until more recent times.

Paxman's was founded in 1865 by James Noah Paxman with two partners named Davey on a site in Culver Street. They commenced trading under the name of Davey, Paxman & Co. Ltd. James Paxman later became a Mayor of Colchester. The firm moved to its present site, the Standard Iron Works at Hythe Hill, in 1876 and the original foundry was taken over by Mumford's Iron Works. Originally, the company's main products were agricultural machinery and steam engines, which were exported to many parts of the world. They later became involved with gas and internal combustion engines. Like so many engineering firms, munitions were made at the factory during the First World War and during the last they were again involved in similar work. The present firm of Paxman's, more correctly called G.E.C. Diesel (Paxman) plc makes diesel engines for a variety of customers including the Royal Navy, oil companies and British Rail, as well as foreign navies. They are currently the largest engineering employer in the area.

Mumford Iron Works established itself in Culver Street and became well known for constructing small steam engines and donkey pumps for yachts. In Victorian times it employed over 150 people. In the 1930s the works were knocked down and a new public library and car park were built on the site. Ironically the library was never fully completed and the land has again been redeveloped. Yet another engineering firm operating at the same time was the Britannia Engineering Company which was next to St Botolph's railway station. This firm produced lathes, woodworking machines and other engineering tools. The premises have now gone and the site is a public car park.

Another local firm of long standing is Woods of Colchester plc, part of the G.E.C. group. The business started in a large corrugated iron shed at The Hythe before moving to their present 17-acre site. They are one of the world's largest manufacturers of electric motors and fans. Other industries existing at the turn of the century included boot and shoe manufacturing, whilst another firm, Leamings, made waistcoats and other clothes using female outworkers who completed the garments at home, supplementing the meagre pay earned by their husbands.

In the early part of the 18th century George Cant had a nursery in St John's Street, then called Gutter Lane. Among the plants he grew were the roses for which he became well known. His grandson, Benjamin Cant, imported improved root stock from France and began to specialise in rose growing with considerable success, with the result that Colchester became famous for its rose trees. His stock and knowledge became much sought after. One of his local projects was to design and lay out Colchester cemetery to a landscape design. A nephew, Frank, started his own business and for a time the two branches of the family went their separate ways, often as rivals and with some bitterness on both sides. Happily, in 1967 the two branches of the family reunited as one nationally-known firm with their main business at Stanway.

The family firm of Pertwee Holdings Ltd. was founded in 1899 by Frank Pertwee in a small warehouse in Back Street just off The Hythe, trading in grains and animal feeds. For Frank it was just a sideline to his main activity as a farmer at Morehams Hall, Frating. In those early days the firm consisted of just two clerks. A friendly coal merchant with a nearby yard took telephone messages on the firm's behalf. Frank's elder son, Norman, joined the firm in 1924 and about the same time the firm moved to the Bridge Granary facing Hythe Bridge. From here the expanding firm was able to purchase larger quantities of maize, taking a load of some 150 tons from a Thames sailing barge which called monthly. In 1944 the firm bought from Unilever – for just over £7,000 –the former Owen Parry Oil Mills further along Hythe Quay. This had been used by the army throughout the war as an ordnance store and was extremely dilapidated. With help from 30 Italian prisoners of war, Norman Pertwee was able to restore the premises and transfer machinery from Bridge Granary. The firm has continued to expand, with the business centred on this property with offices at Harbour House, acquired in 1949 from Paxmans.

The precision engineering firm, Colchester Lathe Company plc, was founded in 1907 on part of the present site by John Ephraim Cohen, the sole proprietor. The original brick building was about 100 feet square and located at the rear of houses then fronting Hythe Station Road. Access was via a right of way known as 'The Chase'. To begin with the new firm faced an uphill battle as it was in direct competition with the older established and larger Britannia Engineering Company, which also produced lathes.

At first the company employed about 50 men, whose harsh working environment was typical of the times. They made four or five lathes a week under gas lighting supplemented by candlelight for close work. A steam-driven turbine engine powered the belt-driven machines. In winter the men gathered at meal breaks around the only form of heating provided – tortoise stoves – and, although strictly forbidden by the management, roasted bacon or potatoes to keep out the cold. The 'Mascot' – one of the first machines to be produced – brought commercial success. It could be powered either by belt, foot treadle or from a two-h.p. electric motor. The Great War brought expansion and the workforce doubled. Despite the subsequent inter-war depression, the company continued to grow in size, employees and range of products. By 1971 the firm was producing over 200 lathes per week. Currently it has the greatest number of Queen's Awards to Industry in the machine tool industry.

Transport

Together with its strategic hillside position, one of the main reasons for the development of Colchester was its position at the head of the Colne, as this tidal estuary was extensively used by the Romans for transportation. It is possible that their main wharves were located in the Middleborough area although there is a theory that they had barge traffic which penetrated considerably further upstream. A series of roads radiated from Colchester from early days. Later, the main stage coach routes from Norwich and Harwich passed through to London along the Great Essex Road, as it was then called. On this road in the 18th century stage coaches like 'The Colchester Eclipse' and 'Harwich Phenomenon' maintained a regular timetable with stopping places at the *Three Cups*, *The George*, the *Red Lion* and other inns.

In the reign of Richard I, the river as far as St Osyth was put under the control of the town, mainly for fishery purposes but also for navigation. A subsequent Act of 1623 gave Colchester better navigation control. In 1719 a pound lock was constructed about half a mile below Hythe Bridge, which created a non-tidal basin at The Hythe. This allowed boats to remain afloat at all times, manoeuvred into different wharves as necessary. By the middle of the 18th century the lock had become ruinous and 100 years later its remains were removed and the river widened and deepened to allow larger craft to use it. Further improvements were undertaken at the end of the 19th century when the river upstream of Hythe Bridge was altered so as to permit sea-going sailing barges to trade to East Mills, rather than relying on lighters. Navigation on this higher section remained a difficult feat as the masts had to be lowered to allow the vessels to pass under two bridges, the boats being poled up on the tide.

Earlier this century Hythe Quay was busy with sailing craft of all types carrying a wide variety of cargoes to and from the town; coal was especially important. There was even a regular steamer service – the *Eagre* and *Gem*. Their captains were Capt. Gentry from Morant Road and Capt. David Francis from Standard Road. Joseph Beckwith owned these two boats and other vessels. In turn, his small fleet was taken over by another local firm, Francis and Gilders. Today, the river remains busy although most of the sailing barges have gone and cargoes are now carried in small, mainly foreign, coasters.

The town's first railway was built in 1843 by the Eastern Counties Railway Company which constructed North Station as the terminus for its line from Colchester to Chelmsford and London. Three years later, in 1846, the Eastern Union Company constructed a line from Ipswich to Colchester and after some negotiations formed an end-on junction with the earlier line at the same station. The decision to butt the two lines together resulted in the creation of tight curves which required a speed limitation for through-trains. This remained a problem until the track was modified in post-war years.

In 1849 the Stour Valley Railway was opened between Sudbury and Marks Tey, with trains continuing over the Eastern Counties line to Colchester. This new track captured much of the trade hitherto carried on river barges from Sudbury to Manningtree, diverting much long-standing coastal trade from Manningtree to Colchester. Earlier, in 1847, the same Company opened a branch line from North Station to The Hythe, with track extending along the quay so as to link up with navigation on the River Colne. Thus a favourable location for industrial development was created. Subsequently, the branch was extended to Wivenhoe, Walton and eventually Clacton, by the Tendring Hundred Railway Company, with The Hythe becoming a passenger station in its own right. The same company built a short branch from The Hythe to St Botolph's, thus creating, for the first time, a terminus almost in the town centre. Nevertheless, it only became important for Walton and Clacton passenger services, and freight and parcels was its mainstay. From time to time, however, it was used as an embarkation point for troop movements to and from the nearby barracks.

All these separate railway undertakings eventually amalgamated into the Great Eastern Railway Company. Subsequently, a further round of mergers took place and the Great Eastern became part of the London and North Eastern Railway. After post-war nationalisation the old Great Eastern re-appeared as the Eastern Region of British Railways. It is currently part of Network South East. In post-war years the extensive steam engine stables at North Station were closed when the various lines were electrified. Freight business has also declined at both St Botolph's and The Hythe.

The Colchester Corporation's Electric Tramway opened on 28 July 1904 but services were confined to the Borough. The vehicles consisted of double-decker trams, with the upper deck completely open to the elements. Each car operated individually and power was provided by overhead cable. The track was laid along the main thoroughfares and the principal routes had a double track down the centre of the road. Lesser routes had a single track with passing places. The trams were painted in a livery of Tuscan red and cream.

The operation was not altogether successful. The steep slopes at North Hill, East Hill and at The Hythe caused considerable operating difficulties and it was not unknown for trams to break down and run backwards down the slopes, to the consternation of the passengers! The system was abandoned in 1927, by which time many of the cars were somewhat decrepit. Although there was talk of replacing them by trolley buses, in the event they were superseded by petrol buses which at first covered similar routes and territory. The Colchester Corporation Transport Department has since expanded to provide a comprehensive bus service to all parts of the Borough, successfully competing with other companies.

The tram tracks, although covered by tarmac, remained in place until the last war when they were removed. Steel was scarce at that time and they were reputedly sent off to help the war effort. Many of the overhead poles erected to support the cable remained in use for some years as lamp standards – the Corporation was also the Town's Electricity supplier. The former tram depot in Magdalen Street is now part of the Corporation's bus depot with a purpose-built bus garage alongside.

Prior to the coming of the railways, all inland movement was by road, and routes to and from Colchester were of considerable importance, with various Turnpike Trusts managing them. Their use greatly diminished with the coming of the railways. However, since the turn of the century there has been a steady transfer of traffic from railways to the roads. Initially, much of this return to road usage was due to improvements to highways. The introduction of tarmacadam saw the end of muddy, deeply-rutted roads. Subsequently the use of reinforced concrete on road surfaces became widespread. Traffic was further encouraged by the development of steam-propelled road vehicles and then by the invention of the internal combustion engine.

At the turn of the century the Great Eastern Railway Company developed bus services from places like Mersea, using heavy, cumbersome, petrol-driven buses which were made at their Stratford workshops. They were timed to act as feeders to the trains. Other companies, however, developed to transport people from one place to another independently of the railways. One such firm was the Chelmsford-based National. Their first vehicles and those of Moore's of Kelvedon, which shared the profitable Chelmsford to Colchester route, were Clarkson steam buses, built at Moulsham Works, Chelmsford. The National expanded rapidly and its first depot at Colchester opened in 1914 but closed due to the war. It re-opened in Queen Street in 1920, on the site of the Theatre Royal. Eastern National, its successor, continues to operate a complex network of services from the town to the outlying communities and elsewhere in Essex.

Other companies included A. W.Berry & Sons, who operated to Mersea and Brightlingsea. They started their operations in 1888, using a horse-drawn bus. Their garage, which housed up to 16 buses, was at the corner of Morant Road and Port Lane. This has since been redeveloped. They were eventually bought out by the Eastern National. Firms with a similar history are Norfolk Buses of Nayland, which ran to and from that village, and Osborne's of Tollesbury which has a service from Colchester to Tollesbury, through to Maldon. Most of these buses ran from the former terminus in St John's Street, today the site of a multi-storey car park.

Public Services

Founded in 1820, the town's general hospital, the Essex County Hospital in Lexden Road, was originally a voluntary hospital. It was set well back from the road in what must have been spacious grounds and enjoyed good views across open countryside as far as Fordham. Early parts were built in a late Georgian style with an Ionic porch over the main entrance. Like most hospitals, it has been continually expanded and wings have been added to the original structure, particularly at the rear.

Infectious diseases coupled with poor sanitation and hygiene were the curse of the last century and the Borough's Isolation Hospital was built at Mile End, then separate and remote from the built-up area of the town. It was hoped that this location would prevent the spread of such illnesses. In 1912, also at Mile End, the County Mental Hospital was established on the edge of the village. It has always been known as Severall's, after the estate on which it was built and patients come for treatment from a wide catchment area. It is also now part of the National Health Service.

Like many other older provincial Municipal Boroughs, Colchester once had its own Police Force, with its authority confined to the Borough. These powers were very jealously guarded. However, the need for specialisation and the greater mobility of the criminal argued against the retention of small police forces and in the early post-war years the town's force was merged with that of the Essex County Constabulary, whose headquarters are at Chelmsford.

Gas production on a small scale began in Colchester in 1817, when Harris and Firman, who ran a chemist's shop in High Street, lit their own premises with gas produced there. This was very successful and they extended the lights along the adjacent street. In due course it became necessary to build a small works in nearby East Stockwell Street. Demand continued to outstrip supply and so a larger works was established on open land at The Hythe, where it was possible to take advantage of water transport for the coal, from which the gas was made. Following the nationalisation of the gas industry by the post-war Labour government, the works at both Chelmsford and Colchester were modernised and linked together for the first time by a high-pressure main, so that one could supplement the other if necessary. The pipe followed the main road and resulted in the closure of several small village works along the route. With the advent of North Sea Gas, production of coal gas ceased and the retorts and furnaces were demolished at both works. At The Hythe today only one of several gasometers built to store the gas remain, and the extensive gasworks site is likely to be redeveloped for other purposes.

Electricity was originally produced in Osborne Street, where the Council opened its own generating plant in 1898. In 1927 a new generating plant was opened at The Hythe, downstream from the gas works. It was able to use the river to import the fuel for the coal-fired furnaces, although rail wagons were also shunted along the quayside from the railway. This plant supplied both the town and the surrounding countryside. In the post-war nationalisation of public utilities both the generation of electricity and its distribution were taken over by nationally-owned undertakings. The generating plant was taken over by the Central Electricity Generating Board and the town linked to the National Grid, with the supply taken over by Eastern Electricity Board.

Military Colchester

Colchester had a long military tradition going back to the Roman era. The Civil War had a permanent impact on the layout and development of the town but the establishment of a camp in Napoleonic times sealed its fate as a garrison town. In 1801 barracks were built at the northern end of a large parade field which stretched from Magdalen Street to Old Heath Road. The army left in 1816 and much of the land was redeveloped apart from a small area of the parade ground which became the recreation ground at the corner of Wimpole Street.

The Army expanded again as a result of the Crimean War and, after the War Office dismissed the idea of establishing a base at Maldon, Colchester was chosen and a new camp was built between Old Heath Road and Mersea Road. Later, Abbey Fields was developed for military purposes. In 1864 an exercise ground was created at Middlewick and a cavalry camp alongside Butt Road. In 1856 a timber-framed and weather-boarded garrison church was added and intended to be used for a limited period only. However, it still remains. Included within the developing complex was a large military hospital but this has now been demolished. Completing the army presence is a military prison, more familiarly known as 'The Glasshouse'. The regime there, at least until recent times, was enough to strike fear into the hearts of any potential miscreants!

With a total area of some 5,000 acres, the army retains a strong presence even today, although with a much lower profile than in the past. Soldiers now normally wear 'Civvies' when off duty and the smart, well-fitting and highly-coloured military dress once seen in every street and every corner public house is now largely a thing of the past. Gone too, except on special occasions, are the ceremonial tattoos and parades, once such a feature of Colchester life.

Large numbers of Colcestrians joined the armed forces in both World Wars. In the Great War, the casualties suffered were particularly heavy and few families were unaffected. In the Second World War young men were again called to the colours and served at home and abroad in all theatres of war. For the first time, however, in English modern history, the war directly affected people on the home front as Colchester was bombed on a number of occasions, although never as frequently or intensively as the county town, Chelmsford, and the Thameside towns. In February 1944, factories plus several shops and houses were destroyed at St Botolph's and, in all, 54 civilians lost their lives as a result of air raids before V.E. day finally came. The town was undoubtedly lucky in not being considered a prime target by the enemy.

Precautions against major attack were, however, made. Among the defences were batteries of anti-aircraft rocket guns, installed in Abbey Fields and manned by local Home Guard units. A decoy ghost town was also created, built of laths and canvas on Mersea mud flats, in the hope that any raider would drop bombs harmlessly in the marshes rather than on Colchester.

Bibliography

Benham, Hervey, *Down Tops'l*
Benham, Hervey, *Last stronghold of Sail*
Benham, Hervey, *Once Upon a Tide*
Benham, Hervey, *Some Essex Water Mills*
Clarke, Vernon, *Essex River Colne* (1979)
Colchester B.C. and E.C.C., *Colchester Town Centre Report May 1968*
Colchester B.C. and E.C.C., *Colchester – An Historic Townscape*
Colchester Borough Council, *Colchester – Official Guide*
Colchester Borough Council, *Colchester Castle*
Crawley, R. J., *et al*, *The Years Between, 1909-1969*, Vols I & II
The Essex Almanac (1865)
Essex County Council, 'Essex Archaeology', 'Essex Countryside', 'Essex County Standard'
Gifford, Phillip, *Colchester as it was*
Gordon, D. I., *Regional History of Railways of Great Britain*
Maling, J. J., *Colchester through the Ages*
Marriage, E., & Son Ltd, *The Annals of 100 years of Flour Milling*
Pertwee, Norman, *Not All Roses all the Way*
Pevsner, Nikolaus, *The Buildings of England*
Shell-Mex & BP Ltd, *The Shilling Guides – Essex* (1964)
Sherry, Peter, *A Portrait of Victorian.Colchester*
Sherry, Peter, *A Grand old Town*
Stephenson, David, *The Book of Colchester*

Miscellaneous
Canals of Eastern England
Industries of the Eastern Counties Business Review (1888-90)
The Story of Hatfields (1886-1986)
100 Up Centenary Story of Colchester & East Essex Co-operative Society

The Plates

The Town

1. High Street. The line of shops known as Middle Row was demolished soon after this sketch was published in 1857. St Runwald's church survived until 1878.

2. High Street after the demolition of Middle Row. The tall square building behind St Runwald's church is the earlier Town Hall which was pulled down in 1899 to make way for the present edifice.

COLCHESTER

REFERENCE

1 King Gods Pump	5 St Nicholas Church
2 Mote Hall	6 All Sainte Church
3 St Peters Church	7 St James Church
4 St Runwalds Church	8 St Giles Church

Drawn and Engraved under the direction of J. Deeton.

SCALE

3. A map of the town in 1803.

4. High Street in Edwardian times. Horse-drawn vehicles wait outside the Town Hall. The newly opened Hippodrome advertises its twice-nightly show.

5. High Street, busy with pedestrians, trams and early motor cars, seen here about 1910 from the top of 'Jumbo', the water tower.

High Street, Colchester I.

6. & 7. Two views of High Street in about 1908. (*Above*) Looking east, a crowd awaits the coming tram. (*Below*) Looking west, the Town Hall towers over High Street. 'Jumbo' can be glimpsed in the distance.

HIGH STREET FROM EAST HILL, COLCHESTER.

8. High Street about 1925, seen from East Hill. The perpendicular tower of St Nicholas church dominates the scene.

9. The famous 'Siege House', before it was elaborately restored in 1905. This late 15th-century house still has timbers pockmarked with Royalist bullets from the 1648 siege.

10. Siege House about 1930. It has changed little today but the passing traffic is now much heavier.

11. Hythe Hill near its junction with Port Lane, about the end of the last century, lined with medieval timber-framed and plastered houses. The street has a leisurely air.

12. The junction of Magdalen Street and Military Road in 1897.

13. The ruins of St Botolph's Priory were not always respected. In the early part of the 19th century they were utilised as makeshift farm buildings.

14. St Botolph's Street in about 1910.

15. The 15th-century gatehouse to St John's Abbey, photographed early this century.

TRINITY STREET, COLCHESTER

16. Trinity Street was a quiet back street when this 'Bull-nose' Morris passed along it earlier this century.

17. Scheregate Steps, *c.*1910. Even then it was an important pedestrian way but with much less bustle than today.

18. Long Wyre Street, well established as one of the town's main shopping streets. The Colchester and East Essex Co-operative Society was established here in 1878.

19. Pelhams Lane, about 1910, then a little used thoroughfare.

20. A glimpse of the Victorian water tower, 'Jumbo', through the arched Balkerne Gate about 1920.

21. St Mary's steps, Balkerne Hill, 1824. Its peace and tranquility, as well as the charming cottage, have all gone, making way for the modern dual carriageway.

22. Head Street in more leisurely times. Then it had a predominantly Georgian character, since much eroded.

23. Headgate early this century. The sparse traffic consists of cyclists and horse-drawn vehicles.

24. Lexden Road in 1904, a dignified tree-lined highway leading out of the town. The overhead wires and massive poles provide evidence of the developing telephone network. Each pair of wires represents a subscriber.

25. North Hill at the High Street junction, about 1910. A tram trundles carefully down the steep slope.

26. A lady and a gentleman prepare to depart in their pony and trap from one of the Georgian-fronted houses midway down North Hill, about 1910.

27. Looking up North Hill. Traffiic lights now control a busy road junction where this photograph was taken early this century, looking up North Hill.

Commerce

28. No. 11 High Street was in Regency times a prosperous grocery shop.

29. Colchester and East Essex Co-operative Society's first clothing and shoe shop in Long Wyre Street, towards the end of the last century. Their modern departmental store now stands on this site.

30. The neatly stacked interior of the Colchester and East Essex Co-operative Society's shop, *c*.1925.

31.   A 1930's lingerie display by the Co-operative Society.

32. & 33. James Dace & Son had branches at Stratford, Romford and
Chelmsford and specialised in sales of sheet music, records and instruments.
Their closing-down sale in Colchester at No. 21 High Street took place in
1935.

PIANOFORTES, HARMONIUMS, and ORGANS, of the very best
description which the London Trade can supply, may be had of

JAMES DACE, Professor of Music,

5, THE GROVE, STRATFORD;
MARKET PLACE, ROMFORD;
NEW LONDON ROAD, CHELMSFORD; and
154, HIGH-STREET, COLCHESTER.

Instruments may also be seen at Mr. BRIDGE's, High-street, Maldon, and
at Mr. MEAD's, High-street, Witham. Tuning throughout the County
Lessons on the Pianoforte, Organ, Singing, &c., at the above addresses, and in
the various Towns on the Great Eastern Railway.

34. A young Arthur Hatfield outside his father's rather dingy secondhand shop at Nos. 31-34 St John's Street, about 1920, where a miscellaneous selection of goods is displayed.

35. Arthur Hatfield with his assistants, Tony and John London, outside the Stanwell Street premises in about 1950. Newly stocked hardware stands side by side with the traditional secondhand items.

VICTORIA BAILEY

30-32 HEAD STREET, COLCHESTER.

A full range of new and attractive Models by HENRY HEATH are now on view at our Showrooms, where a **visit** is respectfully suggested. Correct in style and unequalled for comfort, these becoming styles are in keeping with the HENRY HEATH reputation for the BEST LADIES' SPORTS HATS.

"GOPHER" (Regd.)

Of superfine fur-felt, this Charming Model is suitable for Town and Country wear.   -   -   **Price 30/-.**

Appointed Agent for

HENRY HEATH HATS.

37. The ancient coaching inn, the *Red Lion Hotel*, about 1900. The plaster facade was later removed in places to expose the underlying timberwork.

Red Lion Hotel, Colchester.

38. & 39. Two old established public houses at the turn of the century. (*Above*) The *Castle* on the north side of the River Colne in North Station Road and (*below*) the *Stockwell Arms* in Stockwell Street.

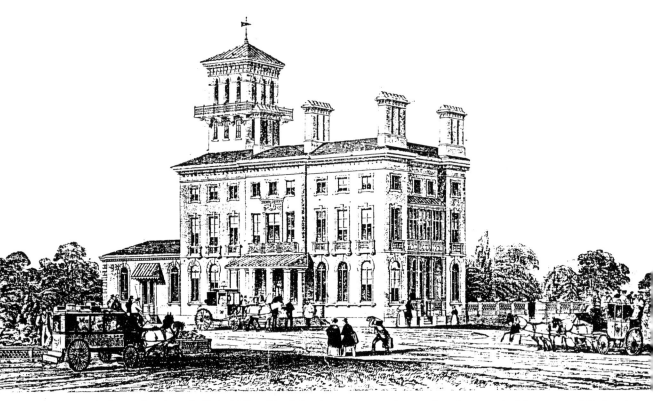

40. This Italianate hotel was built in 1843 at North Station to capture the town's railway trade. The venture failed and in 1859 it became a mental hospital, remaining as such for about a century. It was demolished in 1986 despite efforts to preserve it.

41. The Capital and Counties, a predecessor of Lloyds Bank, owned this substantial building at No. 17 High Street in 1901.

42. The ornate banking chamber at No. 17 High Street.

43. The 1930's Barclays Bank interior contrasts with that of the earlier Capital and Counties chamber, but the expensive panelling and marbled floor was intended to give a similar impression of solid dependability.

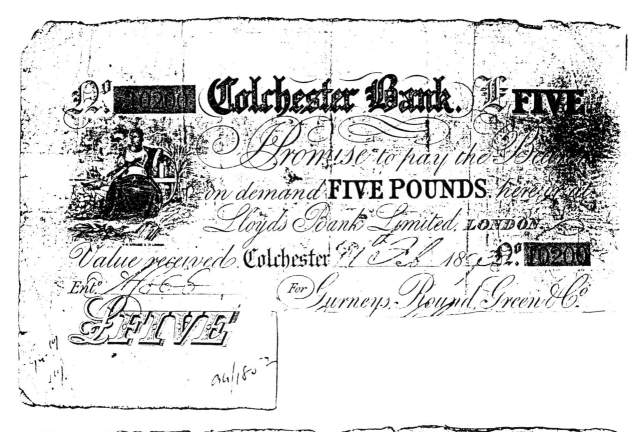

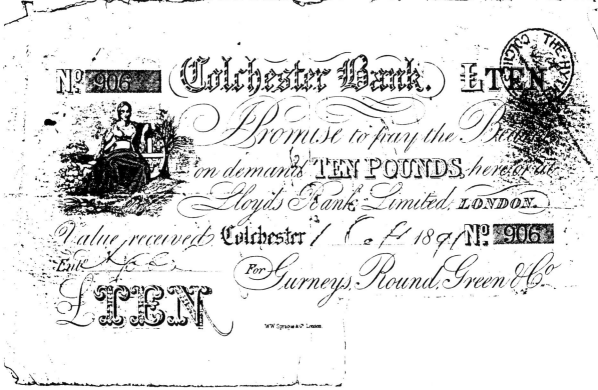

44. Like many other banks in the 19th century, the Colchester Bank (now part of Barclays) issued its own bank notes.

45. This impressive four-storey building at the corner of St Nicholas Street opened in 1899 as a branch of the Warrington-based Parr Bank Ltd. On merging with the Westminster Bank in 1918, the business was transferred to No. 25 High Street.

46. All eyes, animal and human, turn to the camera in this 1900 cattle market scene.

APPEARANCE OF THE FACE WITHOUT TEETH.

THE SAME FACE WITH W.B.'s ARTIFICIAL TEETH

MR. W. BUCK,
DENTIST, 27, HEAD-STREET, COLCHESTER,

HAVING had twenty years' extensive practice in the manufacture of

ARTIFICIAL TEETH,

Has so improved the manner of fixing them on his new

COROLITE OR PATENT GUM

That they can be worn with perfect ease and comfort on the most tender gums restoring mastication and articulation, and with an appearance so natural as to defy the closest inspection to detect their being artificial; they never change color or decay. This description combines all the modern improvements that have been brought out, and is the most economical that can be obtained.

47. An 1865 advertisement extolling the dubious benefits of artificial teeth. Modern preventative dental practice was, alas, many years in the future.

Residential Colchester

48.   West Stockwell Street *c*.1950. Many premises have been renovated but the little shops are now houses.

49. West Stockwell Street earlier in the century, revealing a somewhat run-down appearance with peeling plasterwork.

50. The lower part of the street during the inter-war period.

51. 'Deoban', an elegant house built in fashionable Lexden Road in 1905. Its original owner had retired from the Indian Civil Service and hence special attention was paid to good insulation.

52. Widespread home ownership began after the Great War. The Colchester and East Essex Co-operative Society was a pioneer in providing mortgage advances to members. This beautiful model was displayed on Co-operators Day in 1924 to advertise the Society's work.

The Borough of Colchester ::
Electricity Supply Department

Do you Realise how easily **ELECTRICITY**
can be brought into your home?

WE OFFER YOU

LIGHTING A special domestic cheap all-in tariff
HEATING } At a small fixed charge per quarter
COOKING } Plus ¾d. per unit consumed

MAKE YOUR ENQUIRIES—

Showroom in High St. Telephone 901

THE LARGEST SELECTION OF FITTINGS, FIRE & DOMESTIC :: APPLIANCES TO BE SEEN ::

COOKERS Hired at **4/-, 5/-, 6/-, 7/6** per quarter. Fitted free and maintained.

HOT-WATER CISTERNS Hired at **4/6, 5/6, 6/6** and **8/6** per quarter. Fitted free. **Adequate Hot-Water Supply** for all purposes from **3d.** per day.

"COMPREHENSIVE HIRE-PURCHASE TERMS" for any article or articles over £3 payable quarterly

---

Extra Home Comfort at Small Cost.

Ensure GOOD HEALTH use ELECTRICITY

53. One of the objectives of the 1945 Labour Government was to have electricity installed in every home. In 1928 many town properties were still lit by gas or oil and even then the Corporation was encouraging householders to use electricity.

Schools

54.   Colchester Royal Grammar School was once in Culver Street but in 1853 it moved to premises in Lexden Road. The original buildings still remain in use as part of the present school.

55.   The original Technical School buildings.

BOROUGH OF COLCHESTER

BARRACK STREET, COUNCIL SCHOOL.

Report for the year ending 31st March, 1909, on

Harry Marriage Age _____ Standard V

Quarter.	Possible Attendances	Attendances actually made.	Number of times late.	Position in Class.	Remarks as to character, conduct, and progress.	Teacher's Initials.	Parent's Initials.
1st.	100	100	—	25/45	Conduct Ex. Progress Good.	G.J.	
2nd.	77	77	—	14/48	Excellent.	G.J.	
3rd.	125	125	—	7/49	Excellent.	G.J.	
4th.	115	115	—	17/48	Excellent.	G.J.	

Head Teacher _____

Parents are requested to initial this card and return it to the teacher. At the end of the school year it will become the property of the child. Medal & Prize

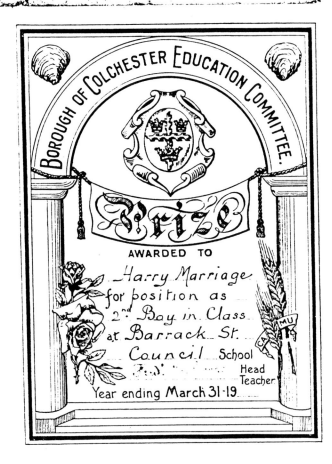

BOROUGH OF COLCHESTER EDUCATION COMMITTEE.

Prize

AWARDED TO

Harry Marriage
for position as
2nd Boy in Class
at Barrack St.
Council School
_____ Head Teacher

Year ending March 31-19____

56. & 57. A 1909 school report. Students who achieved good results were awarded medals and given prizes – usually a book.

58. Pupils of Group XXI, Canterbury Road School.

Open Spaces

59.   Colchester Castle in 1824, then owned by the Round family of Birch Hall. At that time only the southern rooms were roofed, the remainder of the keep being open to the elements.

60. The castle was purchased by Viscount Cowdray for the town in 1920 but it was not until 1933 that the whole keep was roofed over and used as a museum.

61. Castle Park, with an ancient field gun on display, soon after it was opened in 1892.

CASTLE PARK, COLCHESTER

62. Lower Castle Park at the turn of the century, a few years after the ornamental pond was dug. The little boy in the sailor suit was the first of many generations to sail his model boat on its waters.

63. Middle Mill in about 1927 when it was used as a park store by the Corporation. It was pulled down in the late 1950s and a simple weir now marks its site.

Middle Mill, Colchester.

64. The millpond at Middle Mill where a ford existed. It was a popular place to water and cool the horses as well as clean the carts.

65. This attractive little wooden bridge over the River Colne at Castle Park has long since disappeared and has been replaced by a featureless concrete bridge.

Industry

66. Bourne Mill, believed to have been built as a fishing lodge in 1591, was still in use early this century. It is now preserved by the National Trust and is remarkably unchanged.

67. East Mill in 1840, a simple brick and white weather-boarded building, its machinery powered entirely by water drawn from the River Colne.

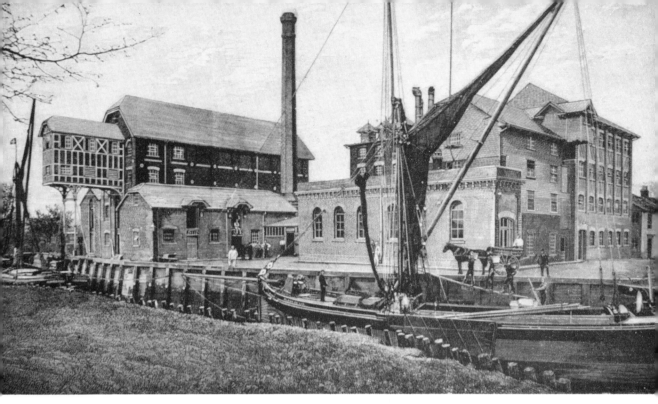

68.   In 1883 part of the original East Mill building was replaced by a brick-clad structure containing a steam roller plant. A granary and stable block was erected at the rear and the river frontage converted into a wharf.

69.   The final complex in about 1940. All trace of the original pretty water mill has gone, to be replaced by a sturdy Victorian industrial building. Milling subsequently ceased at the premises which have now been converted into a hotel.

EXCELLENT FOR ALL HOME COOKING

3 LB. TRADE MARK NET.

REGISTERED

"FELIX"

REGᴰ BRAND

SELF RAISING

FLOUR

MILLED AND PACKED BY

E. MARRIAGE & SON LTD.

(ESTABLISHED 1840)

COLCHESTER & FELIXSTOWE

PLEASE KEEP IN A COOL, DRY PLACE

70. A facsimile of Marriage's 3lb linen flour bag, once a familiar grocery item.

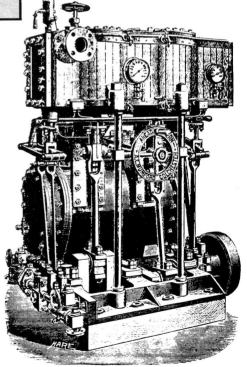

71. A steam pump made by A. G. Mumford at his Culver Street foundry towards the end of the last century.

72. An Ultrasonic steam boiler built about 1930 by Davey, Paxman & Co. Ltd. at the Standard Iron Works at The Hythe.

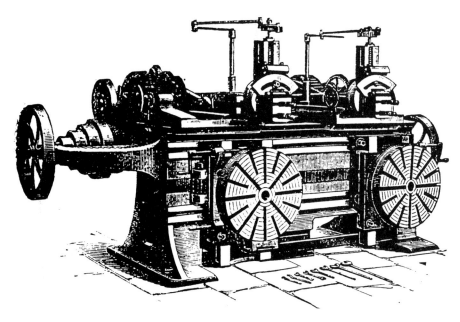

73. This lathe, built about 1890 by the Britannia Engineering Company, appears very clumsy by today's standards but was capable of precision work. Although this company has now disappeared the tradition of making lathes in Colchester is continued by the Colchester Lathe Company plc at their premises at The Hythe.

74. This fascinating aerial photograph, taken about 1950, shows the various industries then at The Hythe. One of the largest sites was occupied by the town's gasworks for which coal was supplied by rail. The largest gasometer was still camouflaged after the war. Years of discarded foundry sand from Paxman's can be seen at the top of the picture.

75. Drying lucerne at Frank Pertwee & Sons premises about 1950. The tower of St Leonard's-at-the-Hythe can be glimpsed through the haze.

76. The massive dust extractor used in the drying plant.

BENJAMIN R. CANT,

ST. JOHN'S-STREET NURSERY,

COLCHESTER,

Has for sale this season a very fine stock of

STANDARD AND DWARF ROSES,

ALSO

FRUIT TREES

OF EVERY DESCRIPTION, WELL GROWN, AND TRUE TO NAME;

ORNAMENTAL TREES;

EVERGREENS, RHODODENDRONS,

AND OTHER AMERICAN PLANTS,

FLOWERING SHRUBS,

GREENHOUSE PLANTS,

VEGETABLE AND FLOWER SEEDS

Of the best Quality, and all at reasonable Prices.

———

SCARLET GERANIUMS, VERBENAS,

AND OTHER BEDDING PLANTS,

CAN BE SUPPLIED IN MAY BY THE DOZEN, HUNDRED, OR THOUSAND, CHEAP.

77. Benjamin Cant's 1865 advertisement for plants on sale at his nursery in St John's Street.

78. The interior of the Colchester Lathe Company's factory in the 1920s, showing gear and hobbing machines to which power was supplied by overhead shaft drive and belting.

79. The 'Mascot', produced by the same company 1914-18. This versatile machine could be powered by pedal, belt drive or an individual electric dynamo.

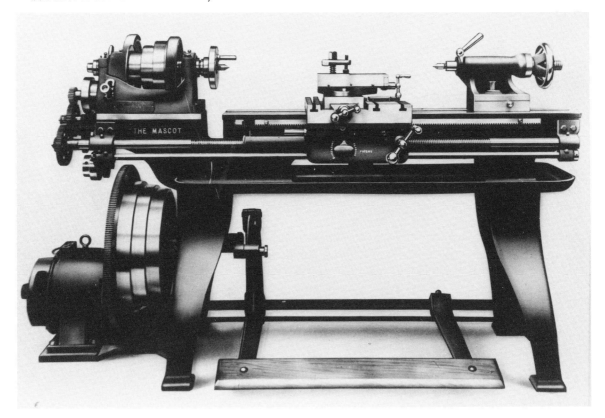

Transport

80. The schooner *Essex Lass* of Colchester plied between England and the Mediterranean with cargoes of fruit and is shown here in 1844 approaching Malta.

81. & 82. Two views of The Hythe in about 1900. Both show the Owen Parry Oil Mills together with Thames barges moored by the quayside. In the photograph above the bow of a schooner can just be glimpsed. Vegetable oil ceased to be produced at the mills in 1932 and they were used during the 1939-45 War as an Army store.

83.   The Hythe in about 1950 with a Pertwee lorry parked next to the Owen Parry gantry. Pertwee's had only recently acquired the mill, and the Thames sailing barge, *Leofleda*, on charter from Francis and Gilders Ltd., was there with a load of cattle food.

84. The Thames sailing barge *Dawn* at East Mills. She was built in 1897 by Walter Cook and Arthur Woodard at Bath Wall Yard, Maldon, for James Keeble. After the Great War she was sold to Francis and Gilders Ltd. for general cargo work. Later, they disposed of their fleet and she went to Brown & Son Ltd. of Chelmsford, who dismasted her and used her as a dumb lighter carrying timber between Osea Island and Heybridge Basin. In 1966 she was acquired by Gordon Swift, who refitted and converted her into a charter vessel. Now owned by the Passmore Edwards Museum of Stratford, she is based at Maldon and occasionally still visits Colchester.

85. *Dawn* passing under Hythe bridge at the start of a long pull up to East Mills.

86. The *Signality* photographed about 1950, departing from The Hythe in ballast. She is typical of the vessel which carries most of the present day cargoes to and from Colchester.

87. The arrival of the first train at North Station from Ipswich in 1846 was greeted by large crowds.

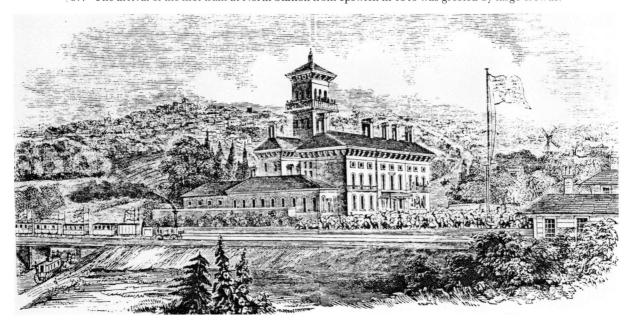

88. The exterior of the original North Station buildings. The station soon proved inadequate for the growing passenger traffic and in 1865 was rebuilt with extra facilities.

89. A London-bound G.E.R. train stands at North Station, with a horse on the track, waiting to move the nearby railway waggons. Horses were once used extensively for shunting purposes.

90. The 11.50 a.m. Colchester to Clacton goods train near North Station on 22 March 1913.

91. A gleaming G.E.R. locomotive takes on water and coal at North Station sidings on 22 March 1913.

92. A tram carefully approaches the High Street-North Hill junction about 1910.

93. A Corporation employee stands ready to change the points at the tramway junction at the top of North Hill.

94. A tram proceeds slowly down steep North Hill to the Station terminus.

95. The driver and conductor pose in front of their tram at the Lexden terminus.

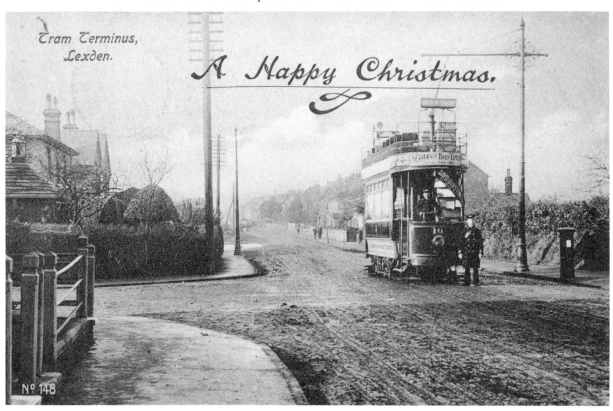

Tram Terminus, Lexden.

A Happy Christmas.

Nº 148.

96. & 97. Two of the buses which superseded the tram services. The open-decked version (*above*) stands outside the present National Westminster Bank and the other outside the Essex and Suffolk Equitable Building. Both photographs were taken in 1929.

98.   A Moore Brothers' bus, *c.*1920. These buses ran a scheduled service between Chelmsford and Colchester in competition with the Eastern National who bought them out in the post-war years.

99.   The interior of the Eastern National bus garage in Queen's Street around 1930 with a collection of double- and single-decker vehicles of varying ages.

100.   The old bus park in St John's Street *c.*1950. Waiting to leave is a Moore's bus with an Osborne's vehicle from Tollesbury parked behind the Eastern National bus.

CHEAP DAY TICKETS

available for Return by

RAIL or ROAD

DAILY

Commencing 2nd February

Chelmsford and Southend and Colchester

Colchester & Dovercourt Bay and Harwich

CHELMSFORD to and from	RETURN FARE 3rd class	
	s.	d.
Southend-on-Sea	3	8
Colchester	2	9
COLCHESTER to and from		
Dovercourt Bay	2	5
Harwich	2	6

AVAILABILITY:

OUTWARD—By any train.

RETURN —On day of issue only by any Train or by the Vehicles of the EASTERN NATIONAL COMPANY, between the points named on the ticket, without extra payment.

Holders of 'Bus tickets between any of the above towns issued by the EASTERN NATIONAL OMNIBUS COMPANY may return on day of issue only by L.N.E.R. without extra payment. Tickets to be exchanged at the Railway Booking Office.

FOR CONDITIONS OF ISSUE, SEE OVER.

London, Jan., 1931.   (P4/1245/16)

101. Towards the end of 1929 the L.M.S. and the L.N.E. Railways gained control of the Eastern National and interchange tickets between buses and trains became possible from 2 February 1931. This valuable facility has, unfortunately, long gone.

EASTERN NATIONAL

(Associated with the L.M.S. & L.N.E. Railways.)

FOLDER OF SERVICES

previously run by

Messrs. A. W. BERRY & Sons Ltd.

Which will be operated by

THE EASTERN NATIONAL OMNIBUS CO. LTD.

as from

THURSDAY, FEBRUARY 18th, 1937.

The Services concerned are as follows :—

COLCHESTER–WEST MERSEA (via Abberton)

COLCHESTER–WEST MERSEA (via Rowhedge)

COLCHESTER–FINGRINGHOE (via Rowhedge)

COLCHESTER–ROWHEDGE

COLCHESTER–BRIGHTLINGSEA

The Time Tables of these Services, which will be continued without alteration, are shown in this Folder in Composite Form with the existing " Eastern National " Services, thus showing together ALL SERVICES which will henceforth be operated by the Company between Common Points.

"Always at your Service!"

THE EASTERN NATIONAL OMNIBUS CO. LTD.

Local Offices :	*Head Offices :*	*Local Offices:*
Queen Street and	**NEW WRITTLE STREET,**	**High Street,**
St. John's Street,	**CHELMSFORD.**	**WEST MERSEA.**
COLCHESTER.	'Phone 3431 (3 lines).	'Phone 17.
'Phone 2449.		

102.   The official notification that the bus services operated by A. W. Berry & Sons Ltd. of Port Lane were to be taken over by the Eastern National.

103. Moore Brothers of Kelvedon ran a general carrier service prior to their bus operations. In this picture, dated about the turn of the century, their cart has at least one passenger in addition to the goods on board.

104. Working horses in stables owned by the Colchester and East Essex Co-operative Society were well managed and this is reflected in their excellent condition. In an age of horse-drawn deliveries these were probably luckier than most.

105. Frank Pertwee and Sons' lorry fleet at the recently acquired Owen Parry Oil Mills in 1947. All their lorries were battleship grey, following a bulk purchase of surplus W.D. paint.

106. Wrights' (Colchester) Ltd. of The Hythe proudly display their new lorry outside their premises in 1920.

Motorists!

SERVICE
For Your Car
Prompt
Efficient
Economical.

Specialists in—
REPAIRS
REPAINTING
WASHING
POLISHING

Oiling and Greasing
ALL SUPPLIES

Service that Satisfies

ADAMS
H. P. Gadsdon **& Co.** 'Phone 200

CULVER ST., —— Colchester.

107. This advertisement appeared in a 1928 guide to the town and reveals the growing influence of the motor car.

Public Building

Town Hall, Colchester

108.   The Town Hall, some ten years after its construction in 1902.

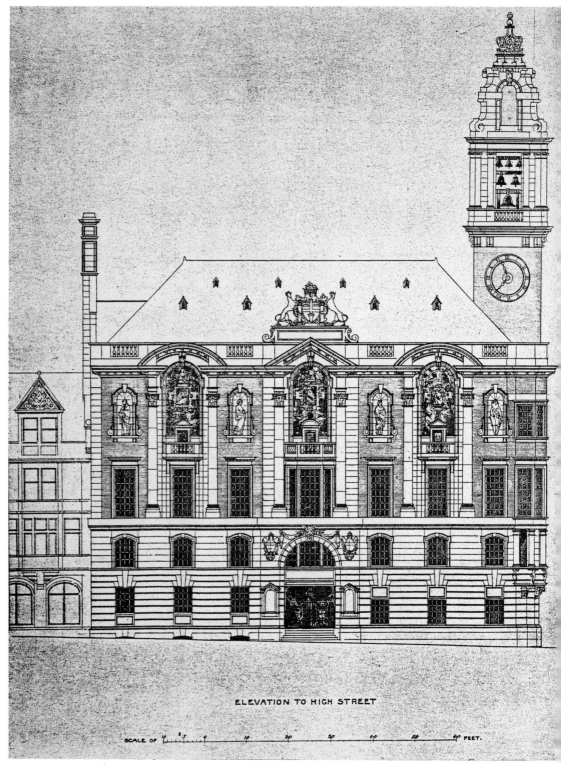

ELEVATION TO HIGH STREET

SCALE OF FEET.

109. After a public competition John Belcher, F.R.I.B.A., was selected to design the present Town Hall. Shown here is the winning entry published in *The Builder*, September 1897. The actual building (*see* plate 108) departed from the plans only in minor respects.

ELEVATION TO WEST STOCKWELL STREET.

SCALE OF .... FEET

110.   Over the years the town has been served by several public libraries. The first was opened in 1894 in West Stockwell Street to a Neo-Jacobean design, the architect being Brightwen Binyon.

111.   This was replaced by a new building, completed in 1939, off Culver Street, designed by Marshall Sisson. The first library subsequently became the Town Hall staff canteen. The second has also been supplanted by a newer building constructed nearby.

112. Colchester and Essex County Hospital dates back to 1820, when it was merely a small two-storey flat-fronted building. This photograph was taken earlier in the present century when various extensions had already been made both at the front and at the rear. Since then further additions have taken place but the frontal appearance to Lexden Road remains remarkably unchanged.

113. The well-equipped interior of the new children's ward at the hospital, opened by Princess Louise in 1908. On the right are high-sided cots for the babies and on the left safe beds with guard rails for the older children. A very ornate lace headed baby's crib and a wooden rocking chair with a sturdy play table, plus cupboards for toys, complete the furnishings.·

Photo by Gill

Essex County Hospital, Colchester.
New Children's Ward.

114. The exterior of the same children's ward. The open-sided glass veranda shows the emphasis placed on fresh air for the patients in their cots and beds.

115. In 1898 the staff of the Colchester Union Workhouse pose for a formal picture just inside the rather Dickensian gates in Popes Lane. It is now St Mary's Hospital under the wing of the National Health Service.

116. St Nicholas church, about 1910. Demolished in 1953, it was replaced by a departmental store of colourless design and little character, much to the chagrin of the locals.

117. Culver Street Methodist church, erected in 1836, was the mother church for a denomination which has strong roots in the town. Like St Nicholas's, it was demolished and its site is now occupied by shops. Its loyal congregation moved to the Castle Methodist church.

118. An artist's impression of Trinity Church as it appeared in the 18th century. It is now within the Lion Walk shopping complex and is used as a museum.

119. The tower of Trinity Church is reputedly Saxon and this photograph shows the unusual triangular topped doorway of Roman bricks.

Military Colchester

Officers' Mess, Hyderabad Barracks, Colchester

120. The Officers' Mess, Hyderabad Barracks, prior to the Great War.

121. A military brass band leads an infantry unit past Company Office, at Sobraon Barracks, about the same time.

122.   Artillery training on Abbey Fields prior to 1914.

123.   Shooting on the ranges and battle training have always been important for both Regular and Territorial units. In pre-war days tented summer camps were common for the visiting militia. A typical camp was one pitched for the 1st Battalion, Hertfordshire Regiment, in 1931. Sleeping accommodation was in the bell tents and the marquees were used as company offices, messes etc.

124.   The Royal Engineers' summer camp, 1912. Sapper Bush (*centre*), from Worthing, assists the cooks preparing the evening meal. Two other soldiers, probably on 'jankers', are peeling the 'spuds'.

SERGEANT: "What is a fine sight?"

PRIVATE RAW: "Two dinners on one plate."

125. A soldier stationed in the barracks in 1917 sent this humorous card to his daughter in Sevenoaks to cheer her up.

126. A studio picture of Gunner Rolly Fisher of the Essex Royal Horse Artillery, May 1916. He later married and lived in Morant Road, serving in the Home Guard during the Second World War.

127. & 128.   Two photographs of the Military Hospital. Busy throughout both wars, it has now been demolished.

129.   Vehicles and drivers of the Army Motor Reserve draw up for review in about 1906.

130.   On 21 February 1915 a Zeppelin raided the town and some damage was suffered. Bombing, of greater severity, was again endured in the Second World War and townspeople were killed.

Historic Events

131. The first sailing barge to reach East Mill in 1865.

132.   In 1884 north and central Essex suffered an earthquake and there was widespread damage. At the *Bell Inn*, Old Heath, workmen make a start on the repairs.

133.   The Police and the Fire Brigade formed a guard of honour at the official opening of Castle Park on 20 October 1892 by the Lord Mayor of the City of London. There was a large turn out of Town Councillors and officials as well.

134. The procession to celebrate Queen Victoria's Diamond Jubilee passes down St Botolph's Street.

135. On 28 July 1904 crowds gathered to watch the opening of the town's new tramway system.

136. The Colchester Fire Brigade proudly display their new steam fire engine outside the Castle entrance, September 1906.

137. & 138.   Colchester pageant depicting the town's history was held in Lower Castle Park from 21 to 26 June 1909 and attracted hundreds of people. H.R.H. Princess Louise also made a visit. The photograph above shows Colcestria and her page boys taking part in the grand march past and the one below depicts Constantius, Helena and King Coel.

139. & 140. On 12 July 1913 at Colchester the Cromer to Liverpool Street express was derailed and a number of carriages destroyed.

141. The unveiling of the War Memorial on Empire Day, 1923.

142. The Colchester carnival has always been a popular summer event. This decorated float appeared in the 1920s.

143, 144 & 145. On 4 July 1924 the Colchester and East Essex Co-operative Society celebrated the annual Co-operators Day with a grand procession which assembled at New Town. The various services offered by the Society were depicted on the floats.

146. The Essex County football team line up at Colchester in 1907 for a photograph before their match against Norfolk.

147. In July 1923 the Fire Brigade tackled a serious fire in High Street. The high timber content of the old building made it a hazardous and difficult task.

Some Colchester People

148.   Viscount Cowdray. As the Rt. Hon. Sir Weetman Pearson he was Liberal Member of Parliament for the constituency from 1895 to 1910. He was a substantial benefactor to the town. Among his gifts were the Castle and Holly Trees Mansion.

149. Wilson Marriage was born in 1842 and succeeded his father, Edward, as the dynamic owner of E. Marriage & Son Ltd. of East Mills. He took a keen interest in town affairs and was Mayor several times.

150. H. H. Fisher (*left*), later to become Mayor of Colchester from 1938-39 and President of the Colchester and East Essex Co-operative Society, is seen here with a friend, Private Harry Marriage, at Winchester in 1917, whilst serving as a private in the 15th London Civil Service Rifles.

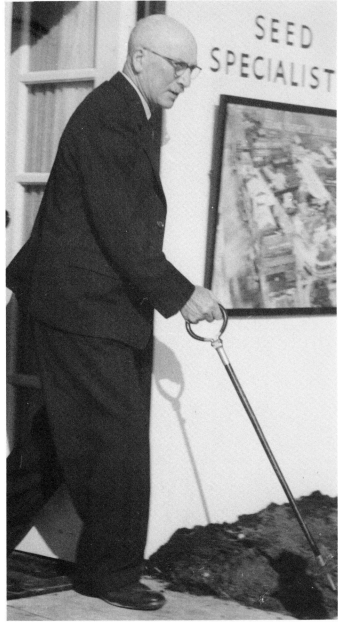

151. John Hatfield, founder of Hatfield Furnishers, at the age of 83, only a few months before he was killed in a motor accident in 1930.

152. Frank Pertwee, who in 1899 started the firm of Frank Pertwee Holdings Ltd. Agricultural Merchants, photographed in the early 1950s at the Essex Show about the time of his 80th birthday.

153. Teddy Grimes and Marmalade Emma, two colourful tramps who roamed the area at the turn of the century. They lived for a time in a hut near Clay Lane.

154. One of the participants of the 1909 Colchester pageant, Jack Clarke aged 14 is seen here in his Rigadoon Dance costume.

155. A young Victorian mother Clara Chambers with her son Victor and daughter Lilly, photographed at the turn of the century in R. Deacon's studio in Queen Street. There was a high rate of infant mortality at that time and Lilly died in childhood.

156.   The entire staff of Colchester Corporation Tramways is assembled here in front of the trams at the depot in Magdalen Street.

157.   A group photograph of the *Essex County Standard* staff about 1930. In the centre sits the editor, William Gurney Benham (later knighted). On his left is a very youthful Hervey Benham, then Editor of the midweek *Colchester Gazette*. In addition to his newspaper interests, Sir Gurney was a prominent local figure and was Mayor three times.

158.   The 1926 wedding of Mabel and Harold Peachey, who later lived in Defoe Crescent, Mile End. Harold was a railwayman all his life.

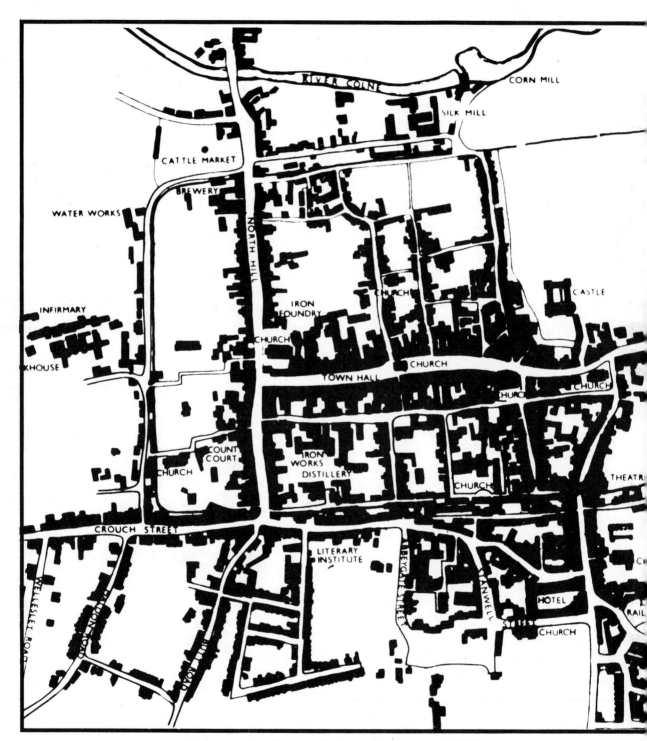

Victorian Colchester, taken from an Ordnance Survey map of 1875.